Art Without Description
I: Ab Initio

Ryan Fredric Steinbeck is the author of ten previous poetry collections:

Soul Ownership	2016
Winter Solstice And What Follows -	2014
Sets In The West	2014
Rises In The East -	2014
Tales Of A Stone Mason -	2013
Inside The Heart -	2011
One House Left Standing -	2009
Hurricane Catherine -	2007
Upper Level Disturbance -	2005
From Darkness Into Light -	2004

Art Without Description
I: Ab Initio

Ryan Fredric Steinbeck

Edited by Shepard Editing
Front cover painting by Conner Smenyak
Cover design by Michael Steinbeck

Published by Ryan Fredric Steinbeck
2019

Copyright © 2019 by Ryan Fredric Steinbeck

All rights reserved. This book or any portion thereof may not be reproduced or used in any manner whatsoever without the express written permission of the publisher except for the use of brief quotations in a book review or scholarly journal.

ISBN: 978-0-578-22341-4

AWD Industries
Chesterton, Indiana 46304

First Printing 2019
Publication Date: 10/26/19

Ordering Information: ryan@ryanfsteinbeck.com

Special discounts are available on quantity purchases by corporations, associations, educators, and others. For details, contact the publisher.

U.S. trade bookstores and wholesalers: Please contact Ryan Fredric Steinbeck: email ryan@ryanfsteinbeck.com

Dedications

For Brenda.

Contents

Square Pegs of Reason, Round Holes of Make Believe 2
One Mind At A Time 3
Something Terrible 4
Currency Of The Spoken Word 5
Under My Breath 6
97% 7
Kill The Lights 8
The Demise of Samuel 9
Up From The Ground 10
City From A Distance 11
Tina Turner In The 70's 12
Replicant 13
Cro-Magnon 14
Lake Ontario 15
Ladakh 16
The Quarry 19
Indifference 20
Arms of September 21
Dark Times 22
Forgiving Sunrise 23
Pendulum 24
A Series of Conversations in One Sitting 25
Ghosts Of The Could've Been 27
Epicentre 28
The Waking 30

A New Dawn	31
Fabulous	32
Amazing Creatures	33
True Love	34
Tidal Waters	35
Butterflies of the World	36
"Love"	37
Warm Sunrise	38
Grateful	39
Oasis	40
Gift Of My Life	41
Super Power	42
Cockroach	43
All In	45

Acknowledgements:

Thanks to Cindy. Thanks to Claire Shepard, Connor and Sarah Smenyak. Thanks to Emily. As always, thanks to Mike R. Steinbeck who has always made the images in my head come to life. Thanks to my teachers, mentors, friends and family.

"With awareness we see,
 with love we accept,
 with wisdom we respond."
— **The Dhamma**

POSTMODERN CHAOS

Square Pegs of Reason, Round Holes of Make Believe

Today it begins again,
everything that was here before,
has been rediscovered,
from the ether my voice of reason returns,
for a final showdown.

When all we thought we had is lost,
new light rises over coastlines of aching,
anger cultivates in roots of action,
unity rises from storms of fear.
the soul's compass points north
despite gales of misdirection.

Our anomalies exposed by microscopes,
reclassified as weakness,
initiators blind to the origin,
humility is not a flaw,
we've always been prone to rebellion,
we cannot be defined or controlled.
We are art without description,
abstractions lost in translation,
puzzles of one million pieces,
square pegs of reason in round holes of make believe.
Our pilgrimage to assimilation,
is a struggle for understanding,
the finest works are imports,
embracing the vastness.
Through the soul we find art,
through art our souls unite.
rising against the odds,
filling the hollows with love,
embracing limitations,
accepting variations,
valuing significance
to the potential of a nation,
to the beauty of creation.

One Mind At A Time

I sense catastrophe beneath the calm sea,
past preconception's rage underneath,
born to rule and consume.
Farewell to the reign,
my voice is fading,
time to roll me like a rug,
throw me into storage,
so the blood in my veins decelerates,
to a hibernation state,
sleep off this mad season,
write off recent history as a lapse of reason.

I'm too high,
the wire's too frayed,
it's not a rush by request,
I'm not at my best.
It's a harsh joke if these dreams are real,
or if the top spinner misspoke,
I'm a fan of the high road,
but I've been going low.

Change human wrongs to human rights,
face darkness with the brightest light,
don't walk away when it's grim,
stand at the foothills,
make the climb,
begin the change,
one mind at a time.

Something Terrible

I ventured into suffering,
when resolve is a flower blossoming,
it comes from something terrible,
rooted in the ground,
metamorphosed in the stem,
how the veins metabolize it,
in the infinite abyss of amazement,
will shape the farewells and helloes.

The flesh is anxious,
thoughts have predecessors,
pioneers are difference makers,
time to be a pioneer.

Currency Of The Spoken Word

I'm thinking through this.
I put my words in a compartment,
ship them to the wordsmith for repairs.
I see no logic in this new way,
I'm nowhere near the source,
they can scream at the tops of their lungs,
I'm doubting anyone cares.

A paragraph of accusations,
allegations and speculations,
I've reached the end of my mind's road,
without leaving the start.

We need the wordsmith to decide,
take what's real and redefine,
dismantle and redesign.
Common sense on the endangered list,
no lifeline back to simpler times or neutral ground,
The currency of spoken word has declined,
reality is nothing more than lost and found.

Under My Breath

I have an expertise,
you asked my opinion,
then disagree with my assessment.
Yes, you're 6'6"
(or so you say)
that only makes you taller,
not necessarily smarter.

We bat topics back and forth,
game, set, match,
ending in a draw.
I smile and pretend I feel no pressure at all,
shake your hand and thank you for your time,
then curse you under my breath as we part ways.

97%

I'm about 97% today,
lately it takes a lot longer to start up,
I monitor my battery icon,
so I don't guess wrong,
or let myself go,
or sleep instead of reboot,
talk instead of shut my mouth.

I feel like an outdated device,
maybe I should be recycled,
I wish I had a 'power off' button,
my biology leaves me with no 'power on' option,
I try to avoid carelessly using minutes,
though it seems to be a skill of mine,
procrastinate until I need a recharge,
save the important updates for another day,
I'm content to roll the dice and believe I'll be around for a while.

Kill The Lights

The ongoing absurdity and paradoxical justifications,
hanging tapestry of feedback,
over your southern humid fly-infested pit,
where your bullhorn sucks in all the localized ears,
as it alters their soundwaves to your frequency,
until you're the only vibration they can hear.

Your inflammatory narrative will light a fire so bright
in the eyes of neophytes and disciples,
it will fill one thousand skies,
as it kills the lights on your proclaimed path of destiny,
so be certain you've plotted your escape,
you won't be leaving the way you arrived.

The Demise of Samuel

The tree tops no longer hold back the morning,
the hour line stalls on the sundial,
the tower clock hands move counter clockwise,
everyone sees the writing on the wall,
no one reads anymore.

The press hinges on every word,
wagering on an early demise,
of the delegated authoritarian,
who quietly skipped town,
with a foreign adversary on speed dial,
pertinent legislature to decide,
in the framework of a system,
fractured by the very architects who built it.

Smog steals the sunset,
dark settles in before it's night,
why is breathing a privilege, not a right?
When the water is gone,
when these monuments fall in flood,
here's some coal to lighten the mood.

He sits atop the eroding mountain range,
all around the world,
there was a time when he remembered her,
before the funding expired,
before the medication ran out,
he misses something he's forgotten,
with tears in his eyes,
he smiles as the last fire on his horizon dies.

Up From The Ground

When I feel subcutaneous,
I cut the skin of the earth,
something subterranean surfaces,
then up from the ground like a bullet to the sky.

This is war,
we are ground zero,
here opinions change with the wind,
officials refute the presence of direction,
denying weathervanes and anemometers exist.

It takes a lifetime to change consequences,
of decisions made in milliseconds,
agendas before a peasant king,
too distracted to read fine print.

Self-appointed, aggrandising,
with a love of divide so wide,
leaving allies on the outside,
he sits on the throne of lies,
looks at his prize,
up from the ground the devil rises to be by his side.

City From A Distance

My apartment has a flower box,
a rose for each family member,
burned in my memory,
a fireplace with the flue closed.

My disclosure on paper,
frail is the feeble mind,
that lives to find damming technicalities,
there's a lost art to being kind.

This city is beautiful from a distance,
the sun glistens off skyscrapers,
as you turn down Main Street,
you start to see the flaws and cracks,
in the transit system,
in faces passing.

Fine print dictates worth,
reliance on an endangered system,
abuses of loyalty and acceptance,
fishing for loopholes,
to put me on a bus,
on a train,
to my country of origin,
where I'm from,
but have never been.

This city from a distance,
on a picture perfect postcard,
will be my only view from now on.

Tina Turner In The 70's

She sang along to everything.
"Proud Mary" was her favorite,
she knew the routine by heart.
From Tina Turner in the 70's,
a role model with class, intelligence, and beauty,
she learned she didn't have to choose.

When you conquer fear,
leave a bad situation,
from "Kings Of Rythm,"
to "A Fool In Love,"
something activated inside when she sang,
when she stood up and said no.

Never the same again,
after Tina Turner in the 80's,
a constant evolution,
a soul that shattered the mould,
she was one in a history of many,
though in bright lights of legacy she stands alone.

Replicant

Wedge yourself comfortably into a preformed mould,
tie the laces of hand-me-down shoes,
run in footsteps of those before you,
invent the originality of imitation,
while celebrants kneel at your feet,
for a moment you feel complete,
before the thrill fades,
the addiction resurfaces,
and you're craving the next complement.
Another step along the path,
in your lifelong pursuit as a replicant.

Cro-Magnon

It's your hour to shine,
for your benign mind,
to be revealed is to be revered,
in this progressive time.

How ideal it is,
the rest of the world moves ahead,
you move back,
sifting through artifacts,
alternative facts,
take a dip in the past,
you baffle the rest,
mostly it's a guess,
or a pretend to know,
just like 40,000 years ago,
it's the Cro-Magnon in your bones.

Despite complete disregard,
and selfish pursuits,
you make the front page news,
nothing but positive reviews,
those of us with twice the vocabulary,
three times the intellect,
are left dumbfounded and confused.

A skull from a different caste,
prehistoric ways on open broadcast,
the chance to quit while your ahead,
is in the past,
despite all prognoses to the contrary,
you thrive and outlast.

Lake Ontario

One day I leapt off the face of the earth,
I disagreed with all that was anything,
then disappeared after the cataclysm.
I can't remember how the world was before,
as I look upon my country from a foreign shore,
mottos and anthems fade away,
we now fight for consolations of war
uniting in protest instead of peace.

I was native to that country,
I believed in something more,
we've been blamed for dissenting,
after enduring disloyalty,
how are we the enemy?

I tug the reigns of forgiveness,
on the horse of violence,
there's still a little give.
I make friends with Lake Ontario,
it's what welcoming used to be,
the way we used to see the world.
It shares its secrets,
reminds me there are still seasons,
still smiles beyond shorelines,
where love and peace are free,
without a master that needs to lead,
here in this nation, in this city,
I'm pardoned for my nationality.

Ladakh

Frayed prayer flags and tapestry,
losing their fight with mountain winds,
stolen times of calm,
life in this high country.

I've been orbiting around the idea for a while,
faint protesting voices down below,
I can't make out their words,
I don't care to.
I'm finished with microscopic dialogue,
I've completed my requisite socializing,
I've observed digressions of nation states,
I've let opportunity slip away.
The time is now,
these borders are closed to international trade,
they still permit my crossing.

I've offered my discretion,
these winds carry a heavy howl,
often times there's loss in translation.
Truth is fleeting,
alternatives are graciously accepted,
I'm veering away from the human element,
looking to the sky mural,
to thinning air where roads diverge,
where country borders meet and no one cares.
The twinkling distant aquamarine lakes,
are diamonds in my eyes.
I've seen enough for now,
to behold a region of synthesized influence,
you'll be greeted by an empty space in my place,
I've distanced myself from the collides of grace.
My desire for relevance suffocates,
my modern day temperament collapses,
if you need me I'll be in the land of high passes.

SGRAFFITO

The Quarry

When I was a kid,
my mother told me not to trespass in the quarry,
after that I couldn't stay away.
Ignorance was bliss.
I was always head over heels for something,
always my own distraction,
misery makes good bedfellows.
I aligned myself with the hidden scar crowd.
I was a gentle storefront,
with a powder keg in the break room,
when I put two and two together,
I realized I cannot pick cherries with my back toward the tree.
So I doubled down,
raised my eyes to the hills beyond my homestead,
departed for eastern trails.
I could see the progression,
the truck departures and arrivals,
the world didn't seem so remote at that moment.

I watched from the gate,
I realized there was nothing here of which to be afraid.
It was a case of playing both ends against the middle,
a fear of exposure,
from a guardian who feared too much,
who thought she could protect me,
from that which was inevitable.
I guess she didn't account for curiosity,
if I never saw the world, maybe I'd never want to leave.
When I find the underlying cause of this,
I was always going to be something,
I was always going to lack something else.
I don't think there was ever a way,
to change any part of the outcome.
I now realize it was a journey to acceptance and letting go,
I don't know if it's ever been fully realized,
but my memories and feelings about the matter,
are all that remain and all I can control.

Indifference

I had a fairy tale youth,
all the while the monstrosity clawed from inside,
every day I'm reminded,
of the ground I covered,
the gaping hole I left.

Our dialogue and excuses,
are tattoos burned onto my brain.
Time riddled my diminishing declarations,
I don't know why I was so angry,
maybe I knew it was time to let go.

Though amnesty found me years ago,
there's still a book of secrets under the bed,
it falls beyond my jurisdiction,
I took a stand by my lack of decision,
for years you demanded I make some sense,
to refrain from denouncing my inheritance,
or admit my obstinacy was incompetence.
I removed walls of semblance,
I've long since rested my defense,
I just can't get beyond my indifference.

Arms of September

The first bonfire of fall,
I follow the trail of ashes to the stars,
in that moment I told you,
it was time to either hold on, or let go.

Like night, you fade into morning skies,
become the first fall rain,
unite with the river,
find the estuary downstream,
as a sediment of a life dispersed to the ocean.

I know you had your doubts about me,
I hope I've proven worthy,
so you can rest peacefully.
The sadness of immediacy,
brilliance of a memory,
magnificence in a private celebration,
of who you were to me,
as you surrender to the arms of September,
into the great mystery.

Dark Times

Dark times can be transformed,
by magnificence of light,
beautiful and bold,
sharp and soft,
fervent,
inviting,
the light lives inside.

Forgiving Sunrise

I am a creature stirring,
my eyes acquire the western skyline,
absorbing morning blue, pink, and yellow,
trees are dark shadow thieves,
stealing my full view.

The morning din of pollution that is us,
dampens my reaction,
so corrupt with intent.
Year wasted chasing aims,
amounting to a single drop in an infinite bucket,
I want to know there's still good in the world,
I hope the emerging day helps me see.

Thoughts eventually merge,
forming drab, grey and black overtones,
satellites of a breaking down dream train,
slowing to a full stop.
Night time silence of despair,
is the nexus to redemption.
A tournament of moonshine and insect songs,
fills me with music of intent,
strings weigh heavy on my heart,
all the years spent aging,
as the wide eyes of time stare me down.
I want to know there remains a plateau of rationality,
to swim in the darkest times with a cannon of levity,
to resolve the unrest of those who have gone before me,
to converse with angels if I am worthy,
I hope the forgiving sunrise forgives me.

Pendulum

Anger fills my lungs,
turn signals and then none,
the rock bottom of patience,
in the driver's seat,
I understand the magnitude,
the reactions,
the repercussions.

Back on the ground,
traveling by foot this time,
peace dissolves frustration,
as if it was never there…
Pendulum.

Heart pounding,
missing home,
a soul flattened on the road,
lack of patience as time erodes.
Wasting hours,
wasting days,
on choices I should've made,
kinks in my life in need of ironing,
brain cells in need of hiring.

Anger at the world for my decision,
curse the sky for my lack of vision,
until I arrive at the door,
see her face…
Pendulum.

A Series of Conversations in One Sitting

We have a strange connection,
in a world where conversation is dying,
skies implode with our goodbyes,
in a series of starts and ends,
we cultivate another topic,
as if the previous never existed.

Deciphering articles of truth from contradiction,
the change in your voice suggests there are many,
your eyes suggest you think the same of me,
there is courage in admittance,
you followed themes of make believe,
long after you realized,
there's no reward for patience.

An interruption by reflection,
brings an intermission,
a sixpence falls in slow motion,
the sound as loud as freight trains.

You've abandoned angels,
drowned demons,
in the era of your cold heart,
where you blissfully stray away in misery,
to find how you returned,
by footsteps in snowfall,
is the most difficult essay to recite.

The sky reciprocated your gesture,
sending you ice before sun,
you waited out the award,
you received the penalty.

When and how we arrived here,
is a mystery box of random letters,
falling on a page together,
a riddle we haven't decoded,

there was nothing else in the universe,
I could ever wish for,
that would compare to the joy in my heart
when we were one in a room of thousands.

The night time forgives us,
for not capitalizing,
for dreaming of day,
I'd planned one hundred responses,
none of them profound,
you juggle words of harsh and kind,
until we find a place to hit rewind,
we rationalize the architecture of our lies,
as we say our last goodbyes,
until some other time.

Ghosts Of The Could've Been

A soul as beautiful as yours,
doesn't deserve the message you received,
the ghosts of the could've been,
the fjords of where you are and what you've seen,
the submergence in between,
swimming in divides,
surface welcoming warmth,
it's only a matter of time,
before it collides with ice beneath.

Epicentre

Goodwill is my epicentre,
like a spider web sprawling,
all corners of the earth,
that shook when she heard the sound,
waves crashing down,
on shores made for her.

My mind lifts from the muck of a drying pond,
wind howls the story of passing hours,
I feel the change to cold,
like it's my last day.
I'm supposed to be the source for her,
so I light my own sky.

A swirling tornado of smoke,
rises over distant treetops,
running from destiny,
all the while she runs toward hers.
The closer she gets,
the higher the water,
the stronger the competitive forces,
obstacles of deterrence defeat me,
not her,
not ever,
she rages like the sea,
rolling like a new-born wave,
a familiar path,
on a foreign journey,
she's everything she always was,
always will be,
a monolithic force to reckon with nature,
here at the epicentre,
I hope my goodwill reaches her.

LIGHT IN DARKNESS

The Waking

The morning sunrise burgeons,
memory threads that manifested,
disperse like water in peaceful springs,
you, my long distance guardian,
will always be part of me.

I needed to be suspended
in my glimpse of the world before,
waiting on the winds to change direction,
now ninety nautical miles from who we were,
in uncharted, yet, familiar territory.
The culmination of a harrowing process,
the harshest tempests spoke on the coldest eve,
"never let the sadness in your life,
cast shadows over beauty."

Universality to singularity,
anchored by the love of many
long after the ice shelf fractured,
color and light refracts through.

Months pose as days,
the artic plateau is my touchstone
debris settles around the temple
for the first time in a long time,
the entire canvass is visible.

I heal inside sacred moments,
like particles of violence solidifying,
what obliterates me rebuilds me.
The prism reveals my past obscurities,
before it shines of all that I am.
No longer in a constant state of breaking,
I rise to the dawn of light,
I ascend to the waking.

A New Dawn

The sky in my dreams as I woke this morning,
I board the last vessel departing the seaboard,
the wind delivers a beautiful new dawn,
on the sonata of an early summer breeze.

Cursing curses until they become blessings,
I take my compass, find my north,
this is my adventure today.
I locate the mainland,
rain passes over to the next state,
the sky an accomplice,
clouds are faces in memoriam,
their farewells in the hum of silence,
crashing waves gather my attention,
until I dock at a new shore.

Patiently waiting,
to reunite with a familiar sky,
knowing the stars are on the opposite side,
the spirit is beside.
Our love was timely,
late to be recognized,
too late to give my hand.
In hurt I blossomed,
learned to feel alive,
you're part of my next breath,
deep in my heart caverns,
in outside voices,
the blind spot of the sun,
the sparkle in water,
the smile of a stranger,
who one day feels like a friend,
soon becomes more.
The part that's over never ends,
just as every soul has origins,
I know this is where love begins.

Fabulous

When you wake up,
the morning rises for you,
speak as the words make you,
walk into night as the stars greet you,
you're fantastic in all that you do,
all that you do is truly you.

It matters not what doors are before you,
you pass through.
Looking back had its time,
it's so yesterday to you.

You drew a line in the sand,
gave yourself a hand,
instead of waiting for the right tune,
you were the instruments and words,
when a path betrays,
you find your own way.

You built a home from a broken heart,
stronger than before,
you don't need a finish line,
it's already a win,
the end is where you begin.
On straits of change,
you were once the sail,
now the wind.

With greatness at a loss to describe you,
every other adjective settles for less,
you're fabulous,
through and through.

Amazing Creatures

She is the neurological chaotic department,
my mind in physical form,
a comically endearing martyr,
an emotionally revolving charade.
She flips through my open scattered catalogue mind,
far from her categorized thoughts,
ready to mobilize in detest,
an intelligent response would take weeks at best,
autonomously hanging on every word,
an amazing creature bordering on manically disturbed.

True Love

Willingly blindfolded,
walk the plank,
depth undetermined,
one foot, then the next,
anticipation to captivation,
elegance in velocity,
gasp reflex
shiver from cold,
descend to the dysphotic zone,
with no more breath to hold,
I'm pulled to the surface.

Through a wormhole,
into darkness,
down a deserted hallway,
ghosts oozing through fixtures,
oblivious like a workday rush,
bumping shoulders,
terror of adjustment,
new surroundings and rules,
an arctic gust through the corridor,
punishing winds across the floor,
a door is boarded up around the corner,
no light trespasses,
the essence of summer evades all obstacles,
its warmth and light find their way through,
this is true love.

Tidal Waters

Winter Island tidal waters,
early summer breeze,
she was told stories about this moment,
forty years in the making.
The ocean greets her eyes,
in a New England state of mind,
her thrill of adventure rises,
like a full moon raising the tide,
hoping joy and memory survive,
until the salty air returns.
She takes it in,
scans the waves and rocks,
reads the coastal narrative,
stories told in a way words could never dream,
inspired by the magic of the sea,
in a realm one could never leave,
yet here she is with me.

Butterflies of the World

In her dream,
she saves the butterflies of the world,
across meadows of color,
surrounding trees are lampposts,
after evening rain.
The sun misbehaves on a podium.

Reach into the warming planet,
lean over cliffs,
mountains to the north,
stormy sea ahead,
eyes fall to tortured rocks below,
she's been lashed by waves of late,
still the calcium deposits build,
like thoughts in her mind.

Overturned leaves have decayed,
their soil impressions remain,
she sells her terms of agreement,
a metamorphosis through thundering meditation.
forgiveness in the dark of night,
under emerging radiance and light,
as it returns to the southern fields of retreat,
the butterflies of the world will finally reunite.

"Love"

I shrug my shoulders to every question,
you roll your eyes to every rebuttal,
you cross-examine my array of contradictions,
annihilate the state of my nation.

I claim distinguished conquests,
you call them cheap parlour tricks,
I could not discern the depth or connotation,
of work to cover a divide,
how long before you would decide,
how smug my gallantry can be,
it was always just love in air quotes to me.

Through an astral ice age,
out the other side,
schlepped some souls with me,
issued refunds for the torment.
My weather-beaten skin,
fragmented piece of mind,
doesn't showcase the depth of the rise.
I won't clear cut your emotional landscape,
or vandalize your spiritual canvass,
I just want something ordinary.

I feared myself devoid of mystery,
petrified of transparency,
until you peel the outer layers.
I acquiesce to subtlety's significance,
domesticate my heart's substance,
release my grip on hindrance.

Outside the world of distractions,
I'm no longer out for effect,
I've honed in on my only truth,
it was always love in air quotes before you.

Warm Sunrise

The orange warming morning sky,
filling my eyes,
blooming across the horizon,
brazen, gritty, peaceful.
In these troubled times,
it's an expression of the hope I feel every day.

Grateful

There was a moment near the end of the song,
when their parts were complete,
they turned their backs to the crowd,
watched and listened as the orchestra brought it home.
He put his arm around his friend and long-time bandmate,
as if to realize again exactly what they have,
what they've accomplished together,
how fortunate they are,
this never is, has been, nor ever will be taken for granted.

Oasis

It was a long, drawn out journey,
I still feel all the scars,
all the pitfalls were real,
I often embellished and hyperbolized them too.
I reach the peak on my own merit,
I find an oasis of originality
hidden in a mountain of parody,
you're a subterranean river,
I'm impermeable rock.
Up here the sun grants illumination,
burns away illusion,
at every turn I am stronger,
without hesitation,
you're a natural wonder,
I'm always curious,
there will never be a time,
when you don't astound me.

Gift Of My Life

You only know truths,
even when it's a disadvantage.
Sleeping on the shortest rides,
reassuring, yet rarely taking my side.
Your unwavering devotion and commitment,
belongs in a simpler time.

Heaven sent,
hell bent,
you're the gift of my life.
Without you I would not be half of what I am.

Super Power

I don't believe I can fly,
I know I can't,
I don't possess x-ray vision,
on Tuesday, Sunday, or any day,
I cannot hurl lightning bolts,
climb walls or spin webs,
nor transform into a giant rage monster during fits of anger.

I can't speak to marine life telepathically,
or run one thousand miles a minute,
I may own a dark past,
I'm not a billionaire vigilante,
I have no ring to harness will power,
nor a lasso that reveals truths,
somehow all of this is moot,
I'm still a hero each and every day,
my super power is you.

Cockroach

Heaven glimmers through smog,
pennies tossed into acid rain wishing wells,
to decide a future,
with distinct, colorless layers.

I'm denied my rest,
as saltwater creeps inland,
trees die from flood,
nothing's real until reaches doorsteps.

Carvings on a cave wall,
illustrates turning fire into light,
we've been here before and persisted,
brash echoes of division are temporary,
love outlasts the before and after.

In a vacuum,
where insurmountable fallacies play out,
with suffocation imminent,
love is air seeping through faulty construction.

Love is surprise and disappointment,
always as intended,
never flawed.

The last hairpin trigger,
for the final detonation,
my city, my town, my lakefront under rubble.
Spirits crushed by hate,
ignorance of fate,
long term moralizing of intellectual stalemate.

Swimming in nuclear waste,
forcing its way to the surface,
bruised and battered, but alive,
love is a cockroach,
it will survive.

When the horizon is here,
when our time has come,
we'll shed our skin and bones,
say our goodbyes,
the absence of endings is revealed,
they could destroy every galaxy,
love is eternal,
it will always be.

All In

Though I'm non-committal on almost everything,
there isn't a second inside my mystified mind,
where it doesn't take my heart to another place.
I'm all in,
you'll always have every single piece.

www.ingramcontent.com/pod-product-compliance
Lightning Source LLC
Chambersburg PA
CBHW031504040426
42444CB00007B/1204